The
UNFOLDING MYSTERIES
of the
VOICE OF THE BLOOD

BENJAMIN AYIM ASARE

Books By Dr. Benjamin Ayim Asare

English Books

1. From Deliverance to Inheritance

2. Life is a Priceless Treasure

3. The Hand of the Diligent Will Rule

4. The Anointing is in the Assignment

5. Discover your Ministry in the Local Church

6. Thanksgiving, A Way of Lifestyle

7. The Unfolding Mysteries of the Voice of the Blood

Italian Books

7. La Vita è un Tesoro Inestimabiled

8. Dalla Liberazione all'Eredità

Available from BENCOM Publications, Amazon.com and Other Retail Outlets

The
UNFOLDING MYSTERIES
of the
VOICE OF THE BLOOD

BENJAMIN AYIM ASARE

BOOK TITLE:
The Unfolding Mysteries of the Voice of the Blood

WRITTEN BY Dr. BENJAMIN AYIM ASARE
ISBN: 978-0-9575775-4-1
eBook ISBN: 978-0-9575775-5-8

First published in Italy in 2018 by **BENCOM**
Via Ghiberti, 1
28100 Novara
Italy

Email: bayimasare@yahoo.it
Email: focicatmissions@yahoo.com
www.benjaminayimasareministries.com

Acknowledgements:
Editing / Proofreading / Research: Dr. Jennifer Pateman
Layout & eBook Marketing: Dorothea Struhlik
Cover Design: Dr.P.
Cover Image Credit: © rfcansole, www.fotosearch.com

❖

Table of Contents

❖

Introduction

God is the source of all life; He existed by Himself from eternity. The origin of the blood covenant and fall of man is a mystery. Blood is a mysterious substance that human faculty cannot comprehend, "The life of the flesh is in the blood" (Leviticus 17:11).

The Scriptures teach that the Son of God, Jesus Christ was slain before the foundation of the world. All who dwell on the earth will worship Him, whose names have been written in the Book of Life of the Lamb slain from the foundation of the world.

So in essence the Blood of Christ is the basic structure that upholds the world. As every solid building depends on the establishment of its foundation, so also the world was established on the Blood of Christ Jesus. The Word of God says, "And according to the law almost all things are purified with blood, and without shedding of blood there is no remission." Blood was accepted by God, as the symbol of the atonement for the soul.

Every flesh has blood and God has given mankind the right to eat the flesh of animals except their blood because the life of the flesh in the blood. Right from the time of Adam, blood has become as a sacred offering to Almighty God.

Abel was the first person who was murdered; the first blood of man that ever stained the soil and there was a cry heard in heaven. God heard the voice of the blood of Abel and the cry was loud, clear and strong for revenge.

All human blood has a voice, therefore whoever slays a person openly or secretly will be exposed one day before the presence of God Almighty because the blood of those people will call for revenge.

The death of Christ is part of the eternal plan of God. This was planned before the world was founded. The death of Jesus Christ was not a spontaneous tragedy or a historical mistake. It was part of a pre-determined plot by the religious leaders of Jesus' day to put Him to death.

They had attempted to kill Him in Nazareth. The high priest Caiaphas predicted the necessity of the death of Jesus (John 11:49-53). They were constantly looking for a convenient time to kill him.

King Herod also wanted him dead. In all of their evil plans, God was in it! The religious leaders and the crowd asked for Barabbas, the murderer instead of Christ, yet it was a determined purpose of God.

The death of Christ was in the predetermined program of God - planned before the foundation of the world. It is a crucial element in God's eternal plan to save humanity from their sins. It was not an accident.

Today, through the shed Blood of Christ, believers have hope in this world and the world to come. The voice of the Blood of Christ is not crying for revenge but cries for mercy. The Blood of Christ speaks better things than the blood of Abel.

As you go through the pages of this book you will discover some amazing truths about the voice of the Blood of Christ, which speaks better things than *anything*.

❖

CHAPTER 1

He Being Dead Yet Speaks

B lood is eternal. It does not die. Blood is sacred unto God. That is the reason why throughout the scriptures He has used blood in various ways to redeem mankind from destruction. The first blood of man that ever stained the soil was Abel's. Abel was dead yet his blood spoke. By faith Abel still speaks, even though he is dead.

The first time blood appears in the scriptures is Genesis 3:21. "And the Lord God made garments of skin for Adam and his wife, and clothed them." When Adam and Eve sinned, God covered their sins with the blood of animals. In this God laid the foundation for animal sacrifices by providing the garments of skin.

In this passage we see the pattern for all salvation history. God took a sacrificial animal, slew it before the eyes of Adam and Eve and wrapped the skins about their naked bodies. No doubt, at that time, God gave them instructions about sacrifice and the covering of sins. God laid down an eternal, divine principle from which there is no deviation.

Adam and Eve were trying to cover up their nakedness or sin by means of fig leaves. Man's finest and noblest efforts can never impress God because He cannot compromise His character. The scripture says, "Not by works of righteousness which we have done, but according to His mercy He saved us, through the washing of regeneration and renewing of the Holy Spirit" (Titus 3:5).

God's absolute righteousness can have nothing to do with man's relative righteousness. When God looks at sinful man He can only reject him. The basis for this rejection is that since the fall of mankind, every human being has been born with an old sin nature and the imputation of Adam's sin; he therefore enters the world spiritually dead, which means no relationship with God.

"That at that time you were without Christ, being aliens from the commonwealth of Israel and strangers from the covenants of promise, having no hope and without God in the world" (Ephesians 2:12).

In the fullness of time, God provided His own perfect sacrifice to cover our sins and provided us with His righteousness. As Christians, we are clothed with His perfect righteousness. We shall go into details about the Blood of Christ in the next chapter.

The animal sacrificed was God's gift and not the work of man, as God gave His Son Christ, as atonement for the sins of the world, so also He provided the animal for the sin of Adam and his wife. This coverage of God on Adam and Eve depicted His future work by the first animal sacrifice – replacing their good fig leaves with divinely good "garments of skin" (Genesis 3:21 NIV).

The Voice of your Brother's Blood Cries out to Me

What have you done? The voice of your brother's blood cries out to Me from the ground.

(Genesis 4:10)

There are a lot of questions that demand an explanation for many believers. People ask why God did not accept Cain's offering, because both of them brought what they produced? Abel brought his offering of the firstlings of his flock and of their fat portions and Cain offered sacrifices that were the labour of his own hands.

I suppose Abel's offering anticipated the coming of the Lamb of God. Abel's offering was a picture of Christ coming to die for humanity. As Isaac, the son of Abraham also was symbolic of Christ Jesus.

As I said earlier, blood is sacred unto God. The blood of Abel was prophetic and pointed forward to that which was to be. The Blood of Jesus, on the other hand, declares that the whole work of salvation is finished. The blood of Abel asked for atonement to be made, the Blood of Jesus declared that the atonement had been made.

The bible says, "By faith Abel offered to God a more excellent sacrifice than Cain, through which he obtained witness that he was righteous, God testifying of his gifts; and through it he being dead still speaks" (Hebrews 11:4).

When Cain killed Abel it was not his spirit that speaks but his *blood.* By faith Abel offered excellent gifts – blood and God declared the good thing that he did, and his blood still speaks. Anything done in faith pleases God.

Faith Pleases God

Faith is the supernatural force that can lead you into the unseen realm. Through faith you can touch the heart of God. Abel pleased God because by faith he brought better offering than Cain did. Abel acted in faith to offer unto the Lord and Cain became jealous and killed him.

Without faith, it is impossible to please God. We are told in the scriptures that, "By faith he (Moses) kept the Passover and the application of the blood, so that the destroyer of the firstborn would not touch the firstborn of Israel" (Hebrews 11:28 NIV).

Friend, you must bear in mind that only faith can touch or please God. In other words, absolutely nothing works in the Kingdom of God outside of faith.

Faith is not just *saying* what God's Word says, but also *doing* what God says, because obedience is better than sacrifice. The scripture says, "For by it (faith) the elders obtained a good report" (Hebrews 11:2 KJV). That means faith is the producer of a good report. Whatsoever things are of good report, think on these things.

Finally, brethren, whatsoever things are true, whatsoever things are honest, whatsoever things are just, whatsoever things are pure, whatsoever things are lovely, whatsoever things are of good report; if there be any virtue, and if there be any praise, think on these things.
(Philippians 4:8 KJV)

It's not how much you know about the Word of God, but how much of the Word inside of you produces faith for exploits. Divine faith is the Word of God abiding in you. It is the Word abiding in you that produces or makes faith. "If you abide in Me, and My words abide in you, you will ask what you desire, and it shall be done for you" (John 15:17).

God cannot be pleased without this fundamental truth we call faith. You see, the Greek word translated faith in the New Testament is *"pistis"* and it is translated as *belief, assurance or fidelity.* God has assured us that He will never leave nor forsake us.

It's on your part to put confidence in Him and know that He who has called you is faithful. Your loyalty to Him is an expression of fidelity. Faith is confidence because if you believe in someone, you have confidence in him.

Faith is obeying, believing, and doing what God says. Faith overcomes every circumstance. In January 2016, after our congregational 7 days of prayer and fasting, I was reflecting on the achievements and failures in the previous year, 2015.

That compelled me to go through all the rent payments of our place of worship. After I summed up seven and half years of rent payments of the church, I was challenged by the huge amount paid for those years.

Suddenly as if someone whispered I heard, "Pray about this issue!" As I began to pray, a Word of God came to my spirit, "For whatever is born of God overcomes the world." I took my bible and read through this page of scripture again and again. "For whatsoever is born of God overcometh the world: and this is the victory that overcometh the world, even our faith" (1 John 5:4 KJV).

After reading and praying my faith was strengthened, boldness and confidence came upon me to seek for a place to buy for the local church. It emerged in my spirit. I began to declare, "My faith has overcome the circumstances; I will buy a place of worship for the Lord."

I did not consider what we had in our coffers or the number of our congregation, (since about 60% of our members had left to other parts of Europe, due to economical crises in Italy), but I looked at the bigness of my God, I put my faith and confidence in Him and every step brought a miracle.

Faith sees the Problem as Privilege

Before all those years our local church had made several attempts to acquire a place of worship, even to an extent that some Italians duped the church. Faith that overcomes the world doesn't look at the challenges but what God's Word is saying.

As I was working towards the vision of a permanent place for the church and somebody I knew directed me to a group of people who owed an old abandoned building, un-roofed and full of trees! Faith sees the problem as a privilege and faith sees beyond the physical realm.

I shared the vision and encouraged the church and simultaneously they responded positively; even though there was much opposition, faith prevailed. Within one year the building was renovated and our local church moved to our own place of worship.

How were we able to fulfil this vision? Because the congregation had a willing heart and were challenged through faith. "This is the victory that overcometh the world, even our faith" (1 John 5:4).

❖

CHAPTER 2

The Voice
of the Blood of the Lamb

The Blood that was shed 2,000 years ago is still speaking. It was appropriate for Him to suffer death so that by the grace of God, He must taste death for everyone. Christ became the pioneer of our salvation, made perfect through the suffering of death.

The reason Christ came in fleshly form is that, "Since the children have flesh and blood, He too shared in their humanity so that by His death He might break the power of death of him who holds the power of death – that is, the devil" (Hebrews 2:14 NIV). So that we can be free from the fear of death.

Our Saviour became like us, fully human in every way, in order for Him to become a High Priest in the service of

God, and to make propitiation for our sins.

> *For the life of the flesh is in the blood, and I have given it to you upon the altar to make atonement for your souls; for it is the blood that makes atonement for the soul.*
>
> *Therefore I said to the children of Israel, "No one among you shall eat blood, nor shall any stranger who dwells among you eat blood."*
>
> *(Leviticus 17:11-12)*

Many people do not understand how blood can take away sins. The bible briefly stated: Since death is the just penalty for sin, the only way God can preserve His righteousness when He forgives sin is if someone else, who is without sin, bears this punishment in the place of the one forgiven. God has given blood as the means of atonement by which sins are forgiven.

> *Being justified freely by His grace through the redemption that is in Christ Jesus, whom God set forth as a propitiation by His blood, through faith, to demonstrate His righteousness, because in His forbearance God had passed over the sins that were previously committed, to demonstrate at the present time His righteousness, that He might be just and the justifier of the one who has faith in Jesus.*
>
> *(Romans 3:24-26)*

Demonstration of Love

Life is in the blood, therefore, blood is life. The blood of Life is in the blood, therefore, blood is life. The Blood of

Christ Jesus shows God's love. "God demonstrated His own love toward us, in that while we were still sinners, Christ died for us. Much more then, having now been justified by His Blood, we shall be saved from wrath through Him" (Hebrews 5:8-9).

But there *is* hope because God, in His great love and mercy, has provided the Blood of Christ as the means of salvation. "And according to the law almost all things are purified with blood, and without shedding of blood there is no remission" (Hebrews 9:22). Our forgiveness came as a result of the Blood of Christ on the cross.

It is the Blood that opened the graves of the dead saints who were held back. When the Blood dropped captivity was broken.

Then, behold, the veil of the temple was torn in two from top to bottom; and the earth quaked, and the rocks were split, and the graves were opened; and many bodies of the saints who had fallen asleep were raised; and coming out of the graves after His resurrection, they went into the holy city and appeared to many.

(Matthew 27:51-53)

When Jesus' Blood was shared on the altar of Calvary – on the Cross the veil of the temple divided into two so that believers can have access to the altar, to apply the Blood of Emmanuel.

When His Blood touched the earth rocks could not stand. Rocks were broken into pieces. Our anchor is the

Blood. Without sacrifice, the altar is useless. By faith I declare the Blood of Jesus Christ upon your life and everything you possess in Jesus' name.

Salvation through the Blood of Christ

Wherefore remember, that ye being in time past Gentiles in the flesh, who are called Uncircumcision by that which is called the Circumcision in the flesh made by hands;

That at that time ye were without Christ, being aliens from the commonwealth of Israel, and strangers from the covenants of promise, having no hope, and without God in the world: But now in Christ Jesus ye who sometimes were far off are made nigh by the Blood of Christ.
(Ephesians 2:11-13 KJV)

The death of Christ was in the salvation plan of God. "He indeed was foreordained before the foundation of the world, but was manifest in these last times for you" (1 Peter 1:20). The death of Christ is part of the eternal plan of God. This was planned before the world was founded. Christ was slain before the foundation of the world for our justification.

So rescuing man from sinful nature was the plan of God. God provides salvation through the Blood of Christ. "For through Him we both have access by one Spirit to the Father" (Ephesians 2:18).

When we realize how sinful man is, and how destructive sin is, we could finally conclude that there is no hope for mankind. But now hope has come to all those who have embraced the salvation plan of God by accepting Jesus Christ as Lord and Saviour. Thus God's grace is granted through the Blood of Christ.

We are "justified freely by His grace through the redemption that is in Christ Jesus, whom God set forth as a propitiation by His blood, through faith" (Romans 3:24-25). "In Him we have redemption through His blood, the forgiveness of sins, according to the riches of His grace" (Ephesians 1:7).

Christ could pay the penalty for our sin because He was without sin. Since He was not under the same condemnation, He could voluntarily take our place. We have now drawn near. The Blood of Christ enables us to stand before God's throne justified:

Then one of the elders answered, saying to me, "Who are these arrayed in white robes, and where did they come from?" And I said to him, "Sir, you know." So he said to me, "These are the ones who come out of the great tribulation, and washed their robes and made them white in the blood of the Lamb."

(Revelation 7:13-14)

What a privilege we have in Christ. Humanity owes God a great debt of gratitude. No amount of money can be able to pay this debt of death and sin.

The Blood of the New Covenant

Covenant is one of the most important concepts and central themes found in the bible. The Hebrew word for covenant is *"brit,"* which appears 284 times in the *"Tanakh"* Old Testament (see Strong's).

This word implies: *pact, treaty, contract* or *agreement between two parties* and is likely derived from the Hebrew verb *"bara,"* which means, *to cut.* The word *"brit" (covenant)* carries a connotation of the shedding of blood.

This is nothing unusual, even from the earliest of times covenant agreements were often ratified by animal sacrifice or the exchange of blood. Such a covenant is so binding that to break it would result in the death of the person who broke it and often the family as well.

We see through the scriptures the various covenant between God and individuals. To mention but just a few, the Abrahamic Covenant:

I will establish My covenant between Me and you and your descendants after you in their generations, for an everlasting covenant, to be God to you and your descendants after you.

Also I give to you and your descendants after you the land in which you are a stranger, all the land of Canaan, as an everlasting possession; and I will be their God.
(Genesis 17:7-8)

In the Abrahamic Covenant, God promised Abraham the land of Israel. Descendants, and blessings, see Genesis 12:1-3. Understanding the Abrahamic covenant is extremely important because it governs God's unique relationship with Israel as well as His relationship with the nations. God's promise of blessing is expanded through the New Covenant.

Behold, the days are coming, says the LORD, when I will make a new covenant with the house of Israel and with the house of Judah — not according to the covenant that I made with their fathers in the day that I took them by the hand to lead them out of the land of Egypt, My covenant which they broke, though I was a husband to them, says the LORD.

But this is the covenant that I will make with the house of Israel after those days, says the LORD: I will put My law in their minds, and write it on their hearts; and I will be their God, and they shall be My people.

No more shall every man teach his neighbour, and every man his brother, saying, 'Know the LORD,' for they all shall know Me, from the least of them to the greatest of them, says the LORD. For I will forgive their iniquity, and their sin I will remember no more.

(Jeremiah 31:31-34)

In fulfilment of the blessings that the Abrahamic covenant would bring to the nations, those who put their faith in Jesus Christ are grafted into the olive tree of Israel. "That the blessing of Abraham might come upon the Gentiles in Christ Jesus, that we might receive the promise of the Spirit through faith" (Galatians 3:14).

And if some of the branches were broken off, and you, being a wild olive tree, were grafted in among them, and with them became a partaker of the root and fatness of the olive tree.

(Romans 11:17)

God promised Abraham that he would be the father of many nations, "Then Abram fell on his face, and God talked with him, saying, 'As for Me, behold, My covenant is with you, and you shall be a father of many nations'" (Genesis 17:3-4).

Through the New Covenant, God has brought all the pieces together that are necessary for the realization of His Son, Jesus Christ who came to share His Blood for all humanity.

When Jesus was speaking with His disciples in the Gospel of John chapter six, He was teaching them the importance of the blood and how His Blood can give life to anyone who will believe in Him.

Then Jesus said to them, "Most assuredly, I say to you, unless you eat the flesh of the Son of Man and drink His blood, you have no life in you. Whoever eats My flesh and drinks My blood has eternal life, and I will raise him up at the last day.

For My flesh is food indeed, and My blood is drink indeed. He who eats My flesh and drinks My blood abides in Me, and I in him."

(John 6:53-56)

When Jesus said, *"Unless you drink My blood,"* He was not referring to the Blood that flowed through His veins – but His nature that was hidden in God before the foundation of the world.

The bible says in the night in which Christ Jesus was betrayed took bread and the cup and declared of the New Covenant in His Blood.

The Lord Jesus on the same night in which He was betrayed took bread; and when He had given thanks, He broke it and said, "Take, eat; this is My body which is broken for you; do this in remembrance of Me."

In the same manner He also took the cup after supper, saying, "This cup is the new covenant in My blood. This do, as often as you drink it, in remembrance of Me."
(1 Corinthians 11:23-25)

We see through the bible how Jesus was about to go to His altar – Calvary. To understand the second Passover (Calvary) we need to understand the first Passover in Egypt.

Now the LORD spoke to Moses and Aaron in the land of Egypt, saying: "This month shall be your beginning of months; it shall be the first month of the year to you. Speak to all the congregation of Israel, saying:

On the tenth of this month every man shall take for himself a lamb, according to the house of his father, a lamb for a household. And if the household is too small for the lamb, let him and his neighbour next to his house take it according to the number of the persons; according to each man's need you shall make your count for the lamb.

Your lamb shall be without blemish, a male of the first year. You may take it from the sheep or from the goats. Now you shall keep it until the fourteenth day of the same month. Then the whole assembly of the congregation of Israel shall kill it at twilight. And they shall take some of the blood and put it on the two doorposts and on the lintel of the houses where they eat it."
(Exodus 12:1-7)

The Passover was God's protection and provision for His people. The blood on the doorposts was for protection, sign for deliverance, not only from death that was passing by, but also from slavery, from Egypt.

"For Christ has not entered the holy place made with hands, which are copies [REPRESENTATIONS] of the true, but into heaven itself, now to appear in the presence of God for us" (Hebrews 9:24). Christ our Passover Lamb went to heaven the same day after the resurrection to show His Blood to the Father and poured that precious Blood on the mercy seat.

The shedding of His Blood provided a permanent sacrifice and a permanent covenant bond between God and man. Friend, you must understand that a priest without a sacrifice is not a priest. That is the reason why the bible says you are also a royal priesthood and that you must offer yourself as a living sacrifice, acceptable unto God, (see 1 Peter 2:9).

The issue of blood is right relationship. To be acceptable, the sacrifice must represent sincere devotion. Therefore, sacrifice without a sincere desire for relationship with God, perverts the real purpose of the sacrificial system and is unacceptable to God. When we come to the throne room of God with the Blood of the Lamb what do we do? God requires a sincere devotion.

Jesus' ministry performed in the true sanctuary, not of earth but of heaven. As Priest and King He occupies the place of supreme power, Jesus' priestly ministrations are endless and changeless, thus enabling Him to bring a salvation that lacks nothing.

Total salvation demands a perfect High Priest and a perfect sacrifice for sins. "Now this is the main point of the things we are saying: We have such a High Priest, who is seated at the right hand of the throne of the Majesty in the heavens" (Hebrews 8:1).

As every high priest offers sacrifice for the people, Christ our High Priest is seated at the right hand of the Father making intercession for us. The first Passover Lamb was a type of Christ and all animal sacrifices in the Old Testament portrayed Christ.

The Passover at Egypt brought deliverance and healing to Israel, so also the New Covenant has provided: *healing, salvation* and *perfect wholeness* to us. "He also brought them out with silver and gold, and there was none feeble among His tribes" (Psalm 105:37).

To Jesus the Mediator of the New Covenant and to the blood of sprinkling that speaks better things than that of Abel. See that you do not refuse Him who speaks.

For if they did not escape who refused Him who spoke on earth, much more shall we not escape if we turn away from Him who speaks from heaven.

(Hebrews 12:24–25)

Jesus becomes the final and perfect High Priest. In the Old Testament, the high priest offered the blood of animals for himself and the nation of Israel as atonement. Atonement is satisfaction for an offense, resulting in the restoration of a broken relationship.

In the New Testament the Blood of Christ Jesus has brought the ultimate sacrifice for sin. "For it is not possible that the blood of bulls and goats could take away sins" (Hebrews 10:4).

The Blood of Christ is for everyone, "They sang a new song, saying: 'You are worthy to take the scroll, and to open its seals; for You were slain, and have redeemed us to God by Your blood out of every tribe and tongue and people and nation'" (Revelation 5:9).

Cleansing by the Blood of Christ is offered to all. In the fullness of time, the LORD God sent His Son Jesus Christ to make atonement for sin once for all. We will go into details regarding the assignment of the high priest in the next chapter.

Let us make some comparisons between the voice of the blood of Abel and Jesus Christ. We see in Genesis 4:10 that Abel's blood cries out and God hears it, then in Hebrews 12:24, the Blood of Christ speaks out and God hears that too.

Abel was a shepherd; Christ is the good Shepherd who gave His life for the sheep. Abel died a violent death at the hand of a relative; Christ died a violent death at the hand of His own nation. Abel *testified* of the righteousness of God, Christ *was* the righteousness of God. Abel died by *force,* Christ died *willingly.*

Abel died *because* of his sacrifice, Christ died *as* the sacrifice. Abel's blood cried for *revenge,* Christ's Blood cries for *forgiveness.* Abel's blood remained on *earth;* Christ's Blood is preserved in *heaven.*

❖

CHAPTER 3

The Perfect Ransom

What is the greatest gift you have ever received? A gift does not have to be expensive to be important. The true value of a gift is not necessarily measured in terms of money. Rather, when a gift brings you happiness or meets a real need in your life, it has great *value* in your life, to you personally.

Those who trust in their wealth and boast in the multitude of their riches, none of them can by any means redeem his brother, nor give to God a ransom for him.

For the redemption of their souls is costly, and it shall cease forever. That he should continue to live eternally, and not see the Pit.

(Psalm 49:6-9)

Some years ago when I was at bible college, I was supposed to buy a particular book to read and to write my thesis within a week, as required by the school, and I was not having the money to buy the book.

I asked my friends for help but it was to no avail. After class one afternoon whilst I was thinking about how I could be able to submit my thesis, a member of our church in Italy called and said, take this number to the Western Union office to collect some money as a gift.

It was to me as a dream; it came at appropriate time to meet my real need in life. It was one of the greatest gifts I have ever received, even though the amount was not too big.

What is a ransom? First, a ransom is the price paid to bring about a release or to buy something back. Second, a ransom is the price that covers, or pays the cost of something. For example, if a person causes an accident, he would have to pay an amount that fully equals to the value of what was damaged.

Adam was a perfect son of God. He was created in the likeness of God. He was without sin and lived not to experience death, he was a perfect man. He committed high treason and all of mankind fell short of the glory of God – all sinned. And amongst the human race, no one was perfect enough to redeem or pay a ransom in order to bring mankind back to God.

"None of *them* can by any means redeem *his* brother, nor give to God a ransom for him, for the redemption of their souls is *costly*" (Psalm 49:7-8). These passages of scripture echo the need for man's redemption.

There needs to be an exchange, or a price for humanity. Do you have something valuable, a purchase price, which you can offer to redeem your soul? The Word of God says, "What will a man give in exchange for his soul?" (Mark 8:37)

> *For what profit is it to a man if he gains the whole world, and loses his own soul? Or what will a man give in exchange for his soul?*
>
> *(Matthew 16:26)*

Since a perfect human life was lost, no imperfect human life could ever buy it back. No one can give to God a ransom - a perfect purchasing price. Billions or trillions of dollars cannot buy the soul of a man. The Blood of the Lamb of God is so much more costly than any other valuable substance.

All the wealth of the world combined cannot redeem even one single soul. Jesus paid for every debt we owed. The bible tells us that Jesus Christ paid for "...the church of God, which He purchased with His own blood" (Acts 20:28).

Human life is very expensive and very precious; life is a priceless treasure. It cannot be purchased with gold or silver. Rich people may think that with their wealth they can buy a person.

Job wondered if there was a redeemer who could stand between himself and God. When Jesus came, His Blood became the ransom for man's redemption. The word ransom means purchase price.

For He is not a man, as I am, that I may answer Him, and that we should go to court together nor is there any mediator between us, who may lay his hand on us both.

(Job 9:32-33)

This passage speaks of the confidence of foolish rich people. The rich people who live without godly principles will die without godly comforts as beasts do - as an animal dies. Job said it's useless for him to make gold his hope and confidence.

"If I have made gold my hope, or said to fine gold, *'You are* my confidence'; if I have rejoiced because my wealth *was* great, and because my hand had gained much..." (Job 31:24-25).

He said to them, "Take heed and beware of covetousness, for one's life does not consist in the abundance of the things he possesses." Then He spoke a parable to them, saying: "The ground of a certain rich man yielded plentifully. And he thought within himself, saying, 'What shall I do, since I have no room to store my crops?'

So he said, 'I will do this: I will pull down my barns and build greater, and there I will store all my crops and my goods. And I will say to my soul, "Soul, you have many goods laid up for many years; take your ease; eat, drink, and be merry."'

But God said to him, 'Fool! This night your soul will be required of you; then whose will those things be which you have provided?' "So is he who lays up treasure for himself, and is not rich toward God."

(Luke 12:15-21)

It is good to have wealth and God is happy with the prosperity of His children. But no human can be redeemed by the abundance of the wealth that he possesses. Money is a legal tender but no amount of value can bring redemption to man.

The Blood of Jesus is the "legal tender" of heaven. But remember, you cannot get anything out of heaven except by the Blood of Jesus Christ, the Lamb of God.

Your good works or your religion is simply not accepted in heaven. The guarantee that stands behind the Blood is the death of Jesus. "And according to the law almost all things are purified with blood, and without shedding of blood there is no remission" (Hebrews 9:22).

You must understand that without faith in the Blood, you have no legal tender:

It pleased the Father that in him should all fullness dwell; And, having made peace through the blood of his cross, by him to reconcile all things unto himself; by him, I say, whether they be things in earth, or things in heaven.

And you, that were sometime alienated and enemies in your mind by wicked works, yet now hath he reconciled in the body of his flesh through death, to present you holy and unblameable and unreproveable in his sight...
(Colossians 1:19-22 KJV)

Real forgiveness of sin is only available through the Blood of Christ Jesus. And it can only be fully realized by experience, not by teaching or ritual. Head knowledge of the availability of forgiveness is insufficient.

But once you experience forgiveness, inexpressible great joy will fill you. Only then, the Blood of Jesus will become a seal on you. God loves us so much that He gave His Son for us, so we could be redeemed:

> *In this the love of God was manifested toward us, that God has sent His only begotten Son into the world, that we might live through Him. In this is love, not that we loved God, but that He loved us and sent His Son to be the propitiation for our sins.*
>
> *(1 John 4:9-10)*

The Great Exchange on the Cross

Jesus tasted death that we might have life; He took the curse that we might have the blessing. In Isaiah 53:4, we find a very interesting word: *"**borne**."* This is the Hebrew word *"**nasa**,"* which means to: *lift up, bear away* or *remove to a distance.*

This is an obvious reference to how the scapegoat carried the sins of the people removing them to a distant place, (see Leviticus 16:8-10; 21-22).

The scapegoat takes the blame. Jesus took our blame; our sickness and this can be called "the great exchange" or "substitution." David said in Psalm 103:3, "Who forgives all your iniquities, who heals all your diseases..."

A cross is a structure for death by crucifixion attached with the victim's name. "And they put up over His head the accusation written against Him: THIS IS JESUS THE KING OF THE JEWS" (Matthew 27:37).

Crucifixion was an ancient method of capital punishment in which the victim was bound alive to a cross. This form of capital punishment was in use among many nations, including the Greeks and the Romans, while stoning was the common Jewish method of execution.

All the men of his city shall stone him with stones, that he die: so shalt thou put evil away from among you; and all Israel shall hear, and fear. And if a man have committed a sin worthy of death, and he be to be put to death, and thou hang him on a tree:

His body shall not remain all night upon the tree, but thou shalt in any wise bury him that day; (for he that is hanged is accursed of God;) that thy land be not defiled, which the LORD thy God giveth thee for an inheritance.
(Deuteronomy 21:21-23 KJV)

His death on the cross has paid the full ransom of our sickness and infirmity. Crucifixion was the most horrible, accursed and shameful death, as we see here in Galatians 3:13, "Christ has redeemed us from the curse of the law, having become a curse for us, for it is written, 'Cursed is everyone who hangs on a tree.'"

Crucifixion was a slow and painful death, usually hastened by breaking the victim's legs (see John 19:31-33). The cross before Jesus' death meant the burden of life.

Pilate said to them, "What then shall I do with Jesus who is called Christ?" They all said to him, "Let Him be crucified!" Then the governor said, "Why, what evil has

He done?" But they cried out all the more, saying, "Let Him be crucified!"

(Matthew 27:22-23)

We see Jesus throughout the entire bible. Let us see a picture of Christ in the Tabernacle God instructed Moses to build, I may not give the full details of the entire Tabernacle but just a glimpse. See Exodus chapters 26 and 27. God instructed Moses to use acacia wood, gold, silver, bronze, scarlet thread etc.

The *acacia wood* represents Christ humility, *gold* speaks of His deity – as a King, *silver* represents our redemption, *and bronze* signifies judgment, whilst *scarlet thread* symbolizes the Blood of Jesus:

You shall make a screen for the door of the tabernacle, woven of blue, purple, and scarlet thread, and fine woven linen, made by a weaver.

And you shall make for the screen five pillars of acacia wood, and overlay them with gold; their hooks shall be gold, and you shall cast five sockets of bronze for them.

(Exodus 26:36-37)

❖

CHAPTER 4

The Assignment of
the High Priest

A priest is someone called or appointed by God to stand between men and God. We, the Church also have been called as Royal Priesthood and Ministers of Reconciliation to rescue people into the Kingdom of our Lord. Therefore our calling or task is to carry out evangelism and missions.

A high priest is a mediator between God and man. Every high priest offers sacrifice on behalf of God and man. So a high priest without sacrifice is not qualified as a high priest. In the Old Testament we see many ways the blood sacrifice has been done between the relationship of God and man. All these were the shadow of what was to come.

The high priest in the Old Testament entered into the holy of holies on the Day of Atonement to offer blood sacrifice for his sins and then the sins of the people. This blood sacrifice was repeated every year as atonement for the people.

The blood of animals provided a temporary atonement or covering for the sins of the children of Israel, but the scripture says, "It is impossible for the blood of bulls and goats to take away sins" (Hebrews 10:4 NIV). So all the blood sacrifice offered was a shadow or a type of the better and perfect sacrifice to come.

Jesus Christ, our perfect and final High Priest, who is the mediator between God and us, shared His Blood on the cross of Calvary and declared, "It is finished!" (John 19:30)

His shed Blood became the eternal covenant to rescue and reconcile mankind back to the Eternal God. In this supreme sacrifice of Christ, the redemption work was completed once and for all to eternity.

For if the blood of bulls and of goats, and the ashes of an heifer sprinkling the unclean, sanctifieth to the purifying of the flesh: How much more shall the Blood of Christ, who through the eternal Spirit offered himself without spot to God, purge your conscience from dead works to serve the living God?

And for this cause he is the mediator of the New Testament, that by means of death, for the redemption of the transgressions that were under the first testament, they which are called might receive the promise of eternal inheritance.

(Hebrews 9:13-15 KJV)

Our Mediator and Intercessor

Jesus is our High Priest who still intercedes for us. He promised us that He would never leave nor forsake us. He promised us His Spirit, the Holy Spirit as a Comforter and Advocate, to strengthen and defend us in all things.

We are living in a world full of evil and it's only because of Him that we are saved. We are kept by the power of God. "Who are kept by the power of God through faith for salvation ready to be revealed in the last time" (1 Peter 3:5). God, in His mercy, has caused His children to be born again unto, "a living hope."

The confidence of the faithful Christian in his future ought to be strong and sure. If we do not live by faith, then there is no power to save us or to keep us saved. If we leave the Lord, then we leave the security He provides. Faith gives courage and confidence to the Christian, when surrounded by temptations and dangers. Faith is the instrument by which means we grasp the divine strength, so that it is made perfect in our weakness. We have a great High Priest:

Since then we have a great high priest who has passed through the heavens, Jesus, the Son of God, let us hold fast our confession.

For we do not have a high priest who is unable to sympathize with our weaknesses, but one who in every respect has been tempted as we are, yet without sin.

Let us then with confidence draw near to the throne of grace, that we may receive mercy and find grace to help in time of need.

(Hebrews 4:14-16 ESV)

We have a real salvation. The former priests were many in number, because they were prevented by death from continuing in office, but Christ holds His Priesthood permanently, because He continues forever. "Consequently, He is able to save to the uttermost those who draw near to God through Him, since He always lives to make intercession for them" (Hebrews 7:25 ESV).

Our High Priest truly meets our needs because He is blameless, holy, and pure and has set apart from sinners and consequently, elevated above the heavens. Christ our High Priest does not need to offer sacrifices day after day for Himself and the brethren. He sacrificed for our sins once for all when He offered Himself on the cross.

Jesus our Perfect High Priest

The biblical role of the high priest is to offer sacrifices and gifts on behalf of the people and God. In the Old Testament the high priest was the supreme religious leader of the Israelites.

Hebrews 8:3 says that, "Every high priest is appointed to offer both gifts and sacrifices, and so it was necessary for this one also to have something to offer." Every high priest has something to offer. Our perfect High Priest is superior to all the high priests under the law.

A high priest under the law had to take the blood of a bull and dip his finger to sprinkle it on the atonement cover seven times and also take the blood of a goat behind the curtain and do with it as he did with the bull's blood to atone for the sins of the Israelites, so also Christ shed His Blood from seven different places of His body.

> *He is to take some of the bull's blood and with his finger sprinkle it on the front of the atonement cover; then he shall sprinkle some of it with his finger seven times before the atonement cover.*
>
> *He shall then slaughter the goat for the sin offering for the people and take its blood behind the curtain and do with it as he did with the bull's blood: He shall sprinkle it on the atonement cover and in front of it.*
>
> *(Leviticus 16:14-15 NIV)*

Christ's head was covered with a crown of thorns and Blood came, a sword went through His ribs, He was wounded from His back, His two hands were nailed and His feet also. Some of His beard was pulled out and He sweat drops of Blood in His agony. Therefore Blood flowed from seven different places of His body (more on this at the end of this chapter).

The high priest sprinkles the blood seven times to empower the altar. It is the blood that empowers the altar. It's the blood that gives power to the altar. An altar without blood or sacrifice is empty. We see it throughout the bible, the mystery of the blood and the altar. The seven places that Blood came out of the body of Christ was a picture of the priest applying the blood seven times.

The Blood of Jesus is our weapon. We are to deploy the mysteries of the Blood against the enemy. It takes the Blood of the altar of Christ to confront all evil powers to surrender. "And they overcame him by the blood of the Lamb, and by the word of their testimony; and they loved not their lives unto the death" (Revelation 12:11 KJV).

Christ is our intercessor. "Therefore He is also able to save to the uttermost those who come to God through Him, since He always lives to make intercession for them" (Hebrews 7:25).

As our High Priest, He always prays for us.

Who then is the one who condemns? No one. Christ Jesus who died--more than that, who was raised to life--is at the right hand of God and is also interceding for us.
(Romans 8:34 NIV)

The Holy Spirit also helps us in our weaknesses in prayer. Often believers find it difficult to pray or intercede for others, but the Holy Spirit takes part with us and makes our weak prayer effective:

Likewise the Spirit also helps in our weaknesses. For we do not know what we should pray for as we ought, but the Spirit Himself makes intercession for us with groanings which cannot be uttered.

Now He who searches the hearts knows what the mind of the Spirit is, because He makes intercession for the saints according to the will of God.
(Romans 8:26-27)

The Acceptable Sacrifice

Then Noah built an altar to the LORD, and took of every clean animal and of every clean bird, and offered burnt offerings on the altar. And the LORD smelled a soothing aroma.

Then the LORD said in His heart, "I will never again curse the ground for man's sake, although the imagination of man's heart is evil from his youth; nor will I again destroy every living thing as I have done."

(Genesis 8:20-21)

The altar of the Lord will not respond to any unclean sacrifice. The covenant of sowing and reaping came as a result of Noah's thanksgiving of clean blood sacrifice on the altar. It is on the altar of Calvary that we received our redemption. It is through the blood on the altar that Abraham had his breakthrough. Almost all things are purified with blood.

Most of the ancestral problems are the issues of evil blood that was shared on evil altars. Many people are living below expectation and have no conscious knowledge of the root of their problems.

And it came to pass, when the sun went down and it was dark, that behold, there appeared a smoking oven and a burning torch that passed between those pieces.

On the same day the LORD made a covenant with Abram, saying: "To your descendants I have given this land, from the river of Egypt to the great river, the River Euphrates."

(Genesis 15:17-18)

47

Blood is life. Blood is eternal and has a voice that can speak of better or evil things. For example, Jacob and his family moved to Egypt not because of the famine that came to the land of Canaan but rather it was the covenant between Abraham their father and God.

It was the power of the covenant, through blood shed on the altar that moved them to Egypt. Why? You may ask. Remember God had a covenant with Abraham that his descendants would be in Egypt for 400 years and at the appointed time He would deliver them.

Then God said to Abram:

> *Know certainly that your descendants will be strangers in a land that is not theirs, and will serve them, and they will afflict them four hundred years. And also the nation whom they serve I will judge; afterward they shall come out with great possessions.*
>
> *(Genesis 15:13-14)*

After 430 years God fulfilled His promise and delivered the descendants of Abraham from bondage - Egypt. Before their deliverance God applied the blood again. He asked Moses to speak to the children of Israel to take for themselves a lamb without blemish according to each household and kill it after fourteenth day on the same month.

They applied the blood on the doorposts of their houses and when He saw the blood, He would pass over them.

> *Now the LORD spoke to Moses and Aaron in the land of Egypt, saying, "This month shall be your beginning of*

*months; it shall be the first month of the year to you. Speak
to all the congregation of Israel, saying:*

*'On the tenth of this month every man shall take for
himself a lamb, according to the house of his father, a lamb
for a household.*

*And if the household is too small for the lamb, let him and
his neighbour next to his house take it according to the
number of the persons; according to each man's need you
shall make your count for the lamb.*

*Your lamb shall be without blemish, a male of the first
year. You may take it from the sheep or from the goats.*

*Now you shall keep it until the fourteenth day of the same
month. Then the whole assembly of the congregation of
Israel shall kill it at twilight. And they shall take some of
the blood and put it on the two doorposts and on the lintel
of the houses where they eat it."*

(Exodus 12:1-7)

God was speaking about the mystery of the Blood of
Christ. You see, it was the power of the blood covenant that
carried the Hebrews to Egypt and it was the blood covenant
that brought them out of Egypt. It was shed blood that sent
Joseph to Egypt.

His brothers envied him, killed him and dipped his
cloth in the blood and lied to their father that a wild beast
had devoured him. They shed the blood of the goat without
knowing that they were fulfilling the purpose and plans of
God!

Jesus' Blood Speaks of Better Things

In the bible, Jesus' Blood speaks of, "better things" and refers to the last days when things will be shaken, so that the things, which cannot be shaken, will remain (Hebrews 12:27). God wants you to know that you will not be shaken when you put your faith in Jesus' Blood, which speaks better things for you.

That is why God wants you to see Jesus' Blood shed for you in every area that causes your heart not to tremble and your confidence not to be shaken. His Blood cries out, so when you are shaken by fears, plead the Blood of Jesus, which cries, "Protection and deliverance will come!" When fear rises in your heart as the doctor gives you bad report, plead the Blood of Jesus over your body. His Blood cries, "Healing and wholeness will come!"

If you are struggling with sin, call upon Him, ask for mercy through His Blood and have faith in Him that there is forgiveness for you and repent.

Therefore, brethren, having boldness to enter the Holiest by the blood of Jesus, by a new and living way which He consecrated for us, through the veil, that is, His flesh, and having a High Priest over the house of God, let us draw near with a true heart in full assurance of faith, having our hearts sprinkled from an evil conscience and our bodies washed with pure water.

Let us hold fast the confession of our hope without wavering, for He who promised is faithful. And let us consider one another in order to stir up love and good works, not forsaking the assembling of ourselves together, as is the manner of some, but exhorting one another, and so much the more as you see the Day approaching.

(Hebrews 10:19-25)

Jesus our Scapegoat

According to the law almost all things are purified with blood, and without the shedding of blood there is no remission of sins (Hebrews 9:22). That scapegoat was symbolic of Christ.

Aaron shall offer the bull as a sin offering, which is for himself, and make atonement for himself and for his house. He shall take the two goats and present them before the LORD at the door of the tabernacle of meeting.

Then Aaron shall cast lots for the two goats: one lot for the LORD and the other lot for the scapegoat. And Aaron shall bring the goat on which the LORD's lot fell, and offer it as a sin offering.

But the goat on which the lot fell to be the scapegoat shall be presented alive before the LORD, to make atonement upon it, and to let it go as the scapegoat into the wilderness.

(Leviticus 16:6-10)

Jesus was in agony, wrestling with the powers of darkness, and suffering his Father's displeasure against the sin of man, for which he was now making his soul an offering "And about the ninth hour Jesus cried with a loud voice, saying, Eli, Eli, lama sabachthani? That is to say, My

God, my God, why hast thou forsaken me?" (Matthew 27:46 KJV)

How to Appropriate the Blood and Oil

Any place the Blood of Jesus is Satan cannot cross or come near. The Blood of Christ is a great protection for Christians. The Blood cleanses us. In the Old Testament the blood was applied seven times in the life of a leper. Lepers are sinners because leprosy stands for sin.

Every sinner must be cleansed or must be brought to the cross for cleansing. All humanity has sinned and all of us need to come to the cross for cleansing. According to the bible in the Old Testament, the priest cleans the leper seven times to make him clean.

The Old Testament priest was a type of Christ and every sinner must come to the priest for cleansing. The leper been cleansed seven times was a symbolic of the work of Calvary. All the duties of the Old Testament priest portrays Jesus Christ, all that they performed or did for individuals, speaks about the work of Jesus on the cross.

In Leviticus 14, we see the picture of the Calvary atonement. The Lord spoke to Moses about the law of the leper, how he can be cleansed. As I mentioned earlier, leprosy signifies sin and before a leper can be cleansed or healed the priest has to apply the blood and oil for atonement.

In this wise, the priest has to take two clean birds, kill one in an earthly vessel over running water. As for the living bird, the priest will take and dip it seven times in the vessel running with water and sprinkles the blood on the leper to be cleansed.

You must understand that the running of the water stands for the Word of God. Jesus said, "That He might sanctify and cleanse her with the washing of water by the Word" (Ephesians 5:26).

> Then the LORD spoke to Moses, saying, "This shall be the law of the leper for the day of his cleansing: He shall be brought to the priest.
>
> And the priest shall go out of the camp, and the priest shall examine him; and indeed, if the leprosy is healed in the leper, then the priest shall command to take for him who is to be cleansed two living and clean birds, cedar wood, scarlet, and hyssop.
>
> And the priest shall command that one of the birds be killed in an earthen vessel over running water. As for the living bird, he shall take it, the cedar wood and the scarlet and the hyssop, and dip them and the living bird in the blood of the bird that was killed over the running water.
>
> And he shall sprinkle it seven times on him who is to be cleansed from the leprosy, and shall pronounce him clean, and shall let the living bird loose in the open field."
>
> (Leviticus 14:1-7)

The two birds speak for Jesus' death and resurrection. The dead bird stands for Jesus' death, whilst the living bird stands for His resurrection. We see through the scriptures that the priest sprinkles the blood on the leper.

First, he applies the blood on the leper's right ear, followed by the thumb of his right hand, then on the big toe of his right foot. Secondly, the priest takes the oil and dips his right finger in it and sprinkles seven times before the Lord and simultaneously, applies the rest of the oil on the right ear, and the big toe of the right foot as he applied the blood. Then the rest of the oil, he puts on the head of the leper to be cleansed.

> *The priest shall take some of the blood of the trespass offering, and the priest shall put it on the tip of the right ear of him who is to be cleansed, on the thumb of his right hand, and on the big toe of his right foot.*
>
> *And the priest shall take some of the log of oil, and pour it into the palm of his own left hand. Then the priest shall dip his right finger in the oil that is in his left hand, and shall sprinkle some of the oil with his finger seven times before the LORD.*
>
> *And of the rest of the oil in his hand, the priest shall put some on the tip of the right ear of him who is to be cleansed, on the thumb of his right hand, and on the big toe of his right foot, on the blood of the trespass offering.*
>
> *The rest of the oil that is in the priest's hand he shall put on the head of him who is to be cleansed. So the priest shall make atonement for him before the LORD.*
>
> *(Leviticus 14:14-18)*

The Blood and the Oil

All these laws of cleansing were a shadow of what would happen on the cross for our atonement and justification. As the blood cleanses the leper and brings healing, so also the Blood of Christ brings atonement and healing to the sinner.

As the priest takes the blood and the oil in his hands and sprinkles each seven times, so also the Blood of Jesus brings salvation, healing and deliverance to the Christian. You must remember that the oil follows the blood; you cannot receive the anointing without the Blood.

First, the cleansing of the Blood – that is our salvation. Salvation comes before the anointing. When a person receives Christ as Lord and Saviour, he then receives the Holy Spirit afterwards. You cannot receive the Holy Spirit without first being saved.

Salvation is a covenant. As it was in the Old Testament, so also in the New Testament – after the leper has been cleansed the priest has to anoint him, and that represents the seal of the Holy Spirit. Likewise, in the New Testament if a person received Jesus Christ as Lord and Saviour, God seals that person by the Holy Spirit to lay claim on him/her as His own.

In Him you also trusted, after you heard the Word of truth, the gospel of your salvation; in whom also, having believed, you were sealed with the Holy Spirit of promise.
(Ephesians 1:13)

The gift of the Holy Spirit to the believer is a down payment on our heavenly inheritance, which Christ has promised us and secured for us on the cross. It is because the Spirit has sealed us that we are assured of our salvation. No one can break the seal of God.

The Holy Spirit is given to us to confirm to us that we belong to the One Who grants to us His Spirit as a gift, just as grace and faith are gifts. Every covenant demands three things: the *Promise, Conditions* and the *Seal.*

Covenants are made between two people: the *promise* is the benefits; the *conditions* are the laws binding the covenant, and the *seal* claims ownership. Without covenant with God, He cannot bless your life.

As blood was sprinkled seven times on the leper who stands as a sinner, likewise Christ bled seven times before and on the cross, to atone for our sins. He became sin for us. "For He made Him who knew no sin *to be* sin for us, that we might become the righteousness of God in Him" (2 Corinthians 5:21).

Let's see quickly the seven occasions and areas of Christ's body that Blood flowed for our redemption:

- **The First:** - His sweat became like blood, *"And being in an agony he prayed more earnestly: and his sweat was as it were great drops of blood falling down to the ground" (Luke 22:44 KJV).* This was for our emotional healing.

- **The Second:** - they whipped His back. The prophet Isaiah declared, *"I gave My back to those who struck Me, and My cheeks to those who plucked out the beard; I did not hide My face from shame and spitting" (Isaiah 50:6).*

  The scripture says, before Pilate released Barabbas to the crowd, Jesus was whipped. *"Then he released Barabbas to them; and when he had scourged Jesus, he delivered Him to be crucified" (Matthew 27:26).*

Barabbas is symbolically you and I, we should have died, we committed the sin of high treason but God released us and killed His sinless Son in our place.

- **The Third:** - Christ bled when a crown of thorns was put on His head and blood covered all His face. *"When they had twisted a crown of thorns, they put it on His head, and a reed on His right hand. And they bowed the knee before Him and mocked Him, saying, 'Hail, King of the Jews!'" (Matthew 27:29)*

- **The Forth:** - they nailed His hands to the cross (see Colossians 2:14). The purpose that His Blood bled from His hands was so that our hands could be blessed with whatever things our hands find to do.

- **The Fifth:** - His feet bled when the nails went through on the cross. It was for our benefit. That we would walk and not faint, and would run and not be weary. Our feet have been anointed to walk on serpents and scorpions to proclaim the Gospel of Peace.

  The Word of God says, *"...How beautiful are the feet of those who preach the gospel of peace, Who bring glad tidings of good things!" (Romans 10:15)*

  And He said to them, *"Go into all the world and preach the gospel to every creature" (Mark 16:15).* With our feet we can take dominion over every place the sole of our foot touches.

- **The Sixth:** - time Christ bled was when the soldier drove a spear into His side to make certain Jesus was dead. *"But one of the soldiers with a spear pierced his side, and forthwith came there out blood and water" (John 19:34 KJV).*

When the spear went through His side, water and blood came, which represents the birth of the Church. The Church is the bride of Christ. Let us go to the book of the beginning – Genesis, to see a very interesting phenomenon.

In Genesis 2:21-23 it says,

"And the LORD God caused a deep sleep to fall on Adam, and he slept; and He took one of his ribs, and closed up the flesh in its place. Then the rib, which the LORD God had taken from man He made into a woman, and He brought her to the man. And Adam said: 'This is now bone of my bones And flesh of my flesh; She shall be called Woman, Because she was taken out of Man.'"

God made Adam's wife from his side and the Church, the Bride (wife) of Christ Jesus, was brought or came out of the side of Christ, when the spear went through Him.

- **The Seventh:** - Christ was bruised. He suffered extensive bruising – that is bleeding on the inside. *"He was wounded for our transgressions; He was bruised for our iniquities; the chastisement of our peace was on Him; and with His stripes we ourselves are healed" (Isaiah 53:5).*

As the Old Testament priest sprinkled the blood seven times on the leper – sinner, so also it can be said that Christ bled His redemptive Blood seven times for us, not just once.

What a victory and privilege we have in God through Jesus Christ our Lord. We find Jesus throughout the bible both the Old and New Testaments.

❖

CHAPTER 5

The Voice
of the Believers and the Martyrs

When He opened the fifth seal, I saw under the altar the souls of those who had been slain for the Word of God and for their testimony, which they held. And they cried with a loud voice, saying, "How long, O Lord, holy and true, until You judge and avenge our blood on those who dwell on the earth?" (Revelation 6:9-10)

Dead men do not go to court but their blood goes to court. Therefore, whosoever kills a person their blood will appear at the court before the Lord. The blood that is shed has a voice – and speaks the language of judgment and not mercy. It does not matter how long blood has been on the ground it will speak because blood does not die.

Therefore the wisdom of God also said, "I will send them prophets and apostles, and some of them they will kill and persecute," that the blood of all the prophets which was shed from the foundation of the world may be required of this generation, from the blood of Abel to the blood of Zechariah who perished between the altar and the temple. Yes, I say to you, it shall be required of this generation.

(Luke 11:49-51)

Jesus declared that to the disciples, "I will build My Church, and the gates of hell (Hades) shall not prevail against it" (Matthew 16:18). Considering these words of Christ, we confirm that His Church will be mightily persecuted and attacked. But one thing we know for sure is that, none of the devil's evil aggressions or attacks can destroy the Church.

Throughout Church history, we see that persecutions against the Church have led many saints to the grave. As the Lord said to the prophet Jeremiah, "They will fight against you, but they shall not prevail against you. For I am with you, says the Lord, to deliver you" (Jeremiah 1:19).

Christ Himself set an example; He was tortured, beaten and crucified on the cross. Every true Church of God will suffer the attack of the enemy. Many times persecution comes from within and without the Church, Satan sometimes works through people in the Church to attack and destroy the purpose and the intent of the Church.

We see throughout the bible that not many years after the Church was born, James a great disciple was murdered.

Now about that time Herod the king stretched out his hands to harass some from the Church. Then he killed James the brother of John with the sword. And because he saw that it pleased the Jews, he proceeded further to seize Peter also...

(Acts 12:1-3)

Satan has been using many people in authority to persecute the Church through out ages. Paul the apostle advises the Church to pray for those who are in authority for the peace in he world we live in.

Therefore I exhort first of all that supplications, prayers, intercessions, and giving of thanks be made for all men, for kings and all who are in authority, that we may lead a quiet and peaceable life in all godliness and reverence.

(1 Timothy 2:1-2)

Stephen, a man full of faith and the power of the Holy Spirit was also killed because of his faith in Jesus Christ; those he was preaching the Good news to murdered him.

When they heard these things they were cut to the heart, and they gnashed at him with their teeth. But he, being full of the Holy Spirit, gazed into heaven and saw the glory of God, and Jesus standing at the right hand of God, and said, look!

I see the heavens opened and the Son of Man standing at the right hand of God! Then they cried out with a loud voice, stopped their ears, and ran at him with one accord; and they cast him out of the city and stoned him. And the witnesses laid down their clothes at the feet of a young man named Saul.

And they stoned Stephen as he was calling on God and saying, Lord Jesus, received my spirit. Then he knelt down and cried out with a loud voice, Lord, do not charge them with this sin. And when he had said this, he fell asleep (dead).

(Acts 7:54-60)

Likewise, Jesus was crucified by His own people; the very ones that He had come to save! Persecution is not past, every day the Christian Church is attacked in various places of the globe, because our enemy, the devil is still roaring like a lion seeking God's children to destroy.

Like Stephen and others who were killed in the name of our Lord, they let their faith, love and courage, touch us to stand for the Gospel of Christ, to rescue those who are perishing.

Your Boldness and Faith can be Seen

"So when they heard that, they raised their voice to God with one accord and said: Lord, You are God, who made heaven and earth and the sea, and all that is in them" (Acts 4:24). As the Lord hears the voice of the blood of innocent people, so also He hears the voice of the believer when you pray.

In the midst of persecution and confusion in the Church of God, we the Christians should ask for boldness to speak the Word of God, as did the early Church. We should ask for the Holy Spirit's empowerment.

The bible describes Peter's dynamic and on-going relationship between the Holy Spirit's power and anointing with the words Peter used to deliver his sermon in Acts chapter three; it was nothing besides his encounter with the Holy Spirit at the Upper Room.

The scripture says they saw his *boldness:* "Now when they saw the *boldness* of Peter and John, and perceived that they were uneducated and untrained men, they marvelled. And they realized that they had been with Jesus" (Acts 4:13). What a description!

❖

CHAPTER 6

Spiritual Assassination

What brings deliverance is your knowledge of the truth of God's Word, not just prayer! Many have become victims in the hands of Satan, due to a lack of knowledge.

In this era of the New Age, there are many people who are still seeking remedy, hope and a better future on evil altars and the demonic world. In this way, Satan has taken advantage of their ignorance, as they shed the sacrificial blood of animals and human beings, in an attempt to appease Satan and his demons.

One of the reasons that Satan can continue to operate effectively on earth - *is blood*. He operates through human beings shedding blood on his behalf.

We know that Satan is a spirit and spirits have no legal right to carry on an assignment, unless they operate though human beings, simply because the earth was given by God, to man.

When God wanted to rescue man from sin and death, He came through His Son Christ Jesus, as a human being, because God Himself is a Spirit and spirits have no legal right to execute an assignment on the planet earth. God died by Himself to redeem man. He paid the price to rescue man.

In this way, Satan uses people for spiritual assassination, ritualism, witches, wizards and cultism etc. And Satan has his own evil priests shedding blood on evil altars, on his behalf.

The assignment of a priest is to offer sacrifice on behalf of the people, to their God (god). It depends which god you are worshipping. We see through scripture just how powerful the blood of animals was during the Old Testament - so how much more the Blood of Christ!

It's the blood that empowers the altar: "For the life of the flesh is in the blood, and I have given it to you upon the altar to make atonement for your souls; for it is the blood that makes atonement for the soul" (Leviticus 17:11).

God gave planet earth to mankind; therefore spirits are illegal to operate on the earth. Since Satan is also a spirit, neither can he operate on this earth, without a human vessel.

Blood is the substance that Satan needs the most, in order to operate effectively on the earth. That is the reason why he works through people to shed innocent blood, against families. He uses evil altars to destroy God's children. You must know that altar without sacrifice is powerless. It is the blood that gives the altar power to speak.

When God delivered Noah after the flood, he built an altar to the Lord and offered clean animals for a thanksgiving. God responded to Noah and pledged that He would not destroy the earth with rain again.

Then Noah built an altar to the LORD, and took of every clean animal and of every clean bird, and offered burnt offerings on the altar.

(Genesis 8:20)

As Satan operated through Cain, to kill Abel, so also he is using many vessels to assassinate people today. Satan has never changed because he cannot repent. He came to kill, steal and to destroy. Lack of the knowledge of the truth of God's Word, gives a right hand to Satan, to destroy.

The Supreme Court of Heaven

There is a tabernacle in heaven where Jesus' Blood is literally sprinkled. It is visible and will be in heaven forever. The Blood was the price paid for our salvation. But for whom was this price paid? He paid for us. Jesus bruised the devil's head at Calvary, for the atrocity that he caused in the Garden of Eden.

And I will put enmity between you and the woman, and between your seed and her Seed; He shall bruise your head, and you shall bruise His heel.

(Genesis 3:15)

The price had to be paid at the court of heaven for us. There was neither bargaining nor debate. It had to be paid in full. Only the divine, shed Blood of Christ would suffice as payment in full. Today, Jesus is seated at God's right hand.

Of course, this is not a progression for Jesus. He was with the Father from the beginning and went back to the Father. He did what He did, so that we could progress.

Satan was judged at Calvary for our justification. The court of heaven sentenced him to life imprisonment.

CHAPTER 7

Our Victory in the Blood

B lood is the foundation of our redemption. Let us take a look at how God orchestrated this magnificent plan to reconcile us to Himself, without Satan's knowledge.

God is in the business of deploying and employing blood throughout history. The foundation of the world was connected and established by the Blood, "The Lamb slain from the foundation of the world" (Revelation 13:8). The Blood of Jesus was not shed 2000 years ago; it was shed before the foundations of the world.

The Blood has been a mystery since the beginning of time. "For the life of the flesh is in the blood, and have given it to you upon the altar to make atonement for the souls; for it is the blood that makes atonement for the soul" (Leviticus 17:11).

When we think of the first sin, we automatically think of Adam but the first sin was not committed in the Garden of Eden. It was committed in heaven by Lucifer, also known as The Morning Star. The sin committed was pride. Lucifer was called a son of God (Job 38:4-7).

Ultimately, he defiled the throne of heaven and was cast down with a third of the angels with him. Now, it is interesting to note that in Revelation 22:16, Jesus is referred to as the *Bright Morning Star*. Morning star means son, and Lucifer lost that status when he thought he could be as big as God.

So after Satan tempted Adam and Eve God laid out the foundation of redemption through the Blood and withheld this mystery from Satan:

And they overcame him by the blood of the Lamb and by the word of their testimony, and they did not love their lives to the death.

Therefore rejoice, O heavens, and you who dwell in them! Woe to the inhabitants of the earth and the sea! For the devil has come down to you, having great wrath, because he knows that he has a short time.

(Revelation 12:11-12)

After the sin in the Garden of Eden man was cut off from the tree of life and a curse was handed down to man separating him from his Creator. God did not want this, but sin will not stay in His presence of pure light.

In Genesis 3:15, God said to the serpent, "I will put enmity between you and the woman, and between your offspring and hers. He will crush your head and you will bruise His heel." The "He" that God was referring to, that would crush Satan's head, was Jesus; so we know from this that God was referring to a singular *Seed,* not many *seeds.*

The ultimate Blood sacrifice and God's Word – *"come in the flesh"* - had been released in the Garden of Eden. The seed of God's Word, Jesus, was hidden in the woman.

> *Then the angel said to her, "Do not be afraid, Mary, for you have found favour with God. And behold, you will conceive in your womb and bring forth a Son, and shall call His name Jesus. He will be great, and will be called the Son of the Highest; and the Lord God will give Him the throne of His father David. And He will reign over the house of Jacob forever, and of His kingdom there will be no end."*
>
> *Then Mary said to the angel, "How can this be, since I do not know a man?" And the angel answered and said to her, "The Holy Spirit will come upon you, and the power of the Highest will overshadow you; therefore, also, that Holy One who is to be born will be called the Son of God."*
> *(Luke 1:30-35)*

From that point God made the Blood a mystery unto Satan. The Blood of Jesus would ultimately purify the heavenly altar that Satan had defiled.

Now if Satan had known this mystery of the Blood, he would have never killed Jesus. "And according to the law almost all things are purified with blood, and without shedding of blood there is no remission" (Hebrews 9:22).

In Exodus 12: 13, we see that blood was the last scene made in Egypt before Pharaoh let Israel go. After Jesus' resurrection, He sent His Blood to the altar in heaven and returned in the same day to the earth until the final ascension. "Gather My saints together to Me, those who have made a covenant with Me by sacrifice" (Psalm 50:5). Without sacrifice there wouldn't be any covenant.

Both Spiritual and Physical death Restored

But of the tree of the knowledge of good and evil you shall not eat, for in the day that you eat of it you shall surely die.

(Genesis 2:17)

The first man rejected God's plan and disregarded the Lord's great warning, but when he bit into that fruit, did he suddenly die? No. Actually, Adam lived for 930 years after he first sinned (Genesis 5:5).

The wages of sin is not *physical* death, "For the wages of sin is death, but the gift of God is eternal life in Christ Jesus our Lord" (Romans 6:23). However Adam did immediately lose his relationship with God, as we saw in the coverage of fig leaves.

Out of fear, Adam tried to hide from the One by whom he had been made alive. In this scenario we see that the wages of sin is *spiritual* death, Adam and his wife died spiritually, the moment that they ate the forbidden fruit.

You see, *physical* death results from *spiritual* death, but *physical* death is never the same as *spiritual* death. For example, if the wages of sin were *physical* death, then the entire human race would have died *physically* at birth, since we are *all* born *spiritually* dead.

The bible is very clear; the entire human race is born with an old sin nature and therefore needs salvation. In order for God to rescue and restore us from *spiritual* and *physical* death, a perfect Man has to purchase our salvation, therefore Christ had to pay the price of both *spiritual* and *physical* death.

So in essence Christ Jesus died twice on the cross. Remember that our Lord was on the cross for six hours, from approximately nine o'clock in the morning until about three o'clock in the afternoon. He was *physically* alive during the entire period, but the three hours from 12:00 noon until 3:00pm was the period of His *spiritual* death. He had no sin of His own. Remember that He came to the cross without *spiritual* death because He had no sin – He was as much alive as Adam was, before the fall.

Christ as a perfect Man hung on the cross, the sins of the whole world were poured out on Him, and the Father judged our sins in Him. This was the *spiritual* death. His substitutionary *spiritual* death was for our salvation.

We see that He was *physically* alive while being judged because He kept screaming, "My God, My God, why hast thou forsaken Me?" (Matthew 27:46). Christ is the only One, throughout Roman history, Who had died twice!

His unique *spiritual* death paid for the sins of mankind and His *physical* death dismissed His own life, in order to complete His assignment and give us the victory over him who has power over death – Satan.

Jesus, our Lord and Saviour gave up His soul and human spirit. This was His *physical* death. "And when Jesus had cried out with a loud voice, He said, 'Father, into Your hands I commit My spirit.' Having said this, He breathed His last" (Luke 23:46).

His human spirit went into the presence of God and His body went into the grave, "Then he took it down, wrapped it in linen, and laid it in a tomb *that was* hewn out of the rock, where no one had ever lain before" (Luke 23:53).

The *physical* resurrection of Christ's body is absolutely essential to the Christian faith:

> *If Christ has not been raised, your faith is futile; (unimportant) you are still in your sins! Then also those who have fallen asleep (dead) in Christ have perished. If in this life only we have hope in Christ, we are of all men the most pitiable.*
>
> *(1 Corinthians 15:17-19)*

Let the Redeemed of the Lord say so

Now if Satan had known this mystery of the Blood he would not have planned to kill Jesus. But in reality it's not Satan who killed Jesus Christ. (He didn't possess power enough, to kill Jesus!) Instead Christ *gave up* His life, for humanity.

Jesus declared that He had the power to *surrender* His life and the power to *take it back up again,* because it was a commandment that He'd received from His Father. Therefore, clearly it was *not* Satan who killed the King of kings.

It is required of every believer to declare from their own mouths, testimony of what the Blood has done for them. It's not enough to read or study the bible, without speaking it out. The Blood that was shed before the foundations of the world - present, past and future.

"Let the redeemed of the Lord say so, whom He has redeemed from the hand of the enemy" (Psalm. 107:2). "Let the redeemed of the Lord *say so*" – means that you should declare or *say* from your mouth (and believe in your heart), what Jesus has done for you.

The Blood is a weapon, especially when your mouth, by faith delivers it. "Let us hold fast the confession of our hope without wavering, for He who promised is faithful" (Hebrews 10:23).

Friend, you don't have to cast away your confidence, which has great reward; your confidence in the Blood is your power. The Lord has redeemed you from the bondage of Satan; we are just passing through this world, like a dangerous and dreary wilderness; often ready to faint through troubles, fears, and temptations.

Sometimes when things go well for people they don't remember the goodness or the power of God. As the bible says, Israel did not remember God. There are many Christians, who if all things work together for good, they stop even coming to church! "They did not remember his power - the day he redeemed them from the oppressor" (Psalm 78:42 NIV).

As we declare the power in the Blood of Jesus and what it has accomplished for us, we will have more confidence in Him. "Therefore, brethren, having boldness to enter the Holiest by the blood of Jesus, by a new and living way which He consecrated for us, through the veil, that is His flesh" (Hebrews 10:19-20).

Confidence to enter God's presence is found in the Blood of Jesus and His High Priestly ministry. Through the Blood of Jesus Christ we were set free from every satanic prison. "As for you also, because of the blood of your covenant, I will set your prisoners free from the waterless pit" (Zechariah 9:11).

For there are three that bear witness in heaven: the Father, the Word, and the Holy Spirit; and these three are one. And there are three that bear witness on earth: the Spirit, the water, and the blood; and these three agree as one.
(1 John 5:7-8)

What Jesus' Blood says to us?

Our victory is in the Blood. The Blood is legal and binding. We understand what the Blood of Jesus means to the believer. Let's see just some of what the Blood of Jesus Christ has done on our behalf:

1. We are justified by His Blood – Romans 5:9

2. We are redeemed through His Blood – Ephesians 1:7

3. We have peace through His Blood – Colossians 1:20

4. We are sanctified by His Blood – Hebrews 13:12

5. We are cleansed from all sin by His Blood – 1 John 1:7

6. We have eternal salvation through His Blood – Hebrews 13:20-21

7. We are washed in the Blood of Jesus – Revelation 1:5

8. We have victory by the Blood of Jesus – Revelation 12:11

Through the redemption work of Christ, we can live a totally victorious life. We have lived for so long in the natural that we are familiar with natural laws and how they work. We must know that God's covenants are governed by supernatural laws and workings.

We can learn to live and adapt to the supernatural world of the Holy Spirit. No longer are we strangers to the covenant of promise:

> *That at the time you were without Christ, being aliens from the commonwealth of Israel and strangers from the covenants of promise, having no hope and without God in the world. But now in Christ Jesus you who once were far off have been brought near by the Blood of Christ.*
> *(Ephesians 2:12-13)*

There is Freedom and New Life in the Blood

As I have said before, it was through the blood covenant that the nation of Israel went to Egypt for over 400 years. And it was through the blood that they were delivered. We read in Exodus 12:7, that the Israelites were instructed to put the blood of the first Passover lamb on the doorposts.

In the next verse, God also commanded them to eat the flesh of the lamb. The Jewish Passover lamb was for protection from Egypt. We know that something took place in their lives when they ate the Passover.

The bible says there was no one weak among them throughout their journey in the desert. God was man's healer, "Jehovah Rapha," "…for I am the Lord who heals you" (Exodus 15:26).

Jesus is our Passover Lamb. We can also expect the same experience that the Israelites had: protection, deliverance, healing and provision.

In the New Testament times, God is man's healer through Jesus Christ:

How God anointed Jesus of Nazareth with the Holy Spirit and with power, who went about doing good and healing all who were oppressed by the devil, for God was with Him.

(Acts 10:38)

In 1 Corinthians 5:7, scripture is clear that Christ was our Passover Lamb who died for our diseases when He died for our sins. Salvation, freedom, health, promotion, protection, and deliverance belong to us. What do we do to experience salvation personally? Believe in His Word; believe in Jesus that He is good enough to fulfil His Word.

Sin is the manifestation of spiritual death in the heart of man. Sickness is the manifestation of spiritual death in the body of man. Jesus came to destroy both sin and sickness.

We have seen from the Word of God that the Church of Jesus Christ has been made just as free from sickness as from sin.

A Christian can continue to sin after he has been born again, but he doesn't have to sin! "For sin shall not have dominion over you, for you are not under law but under grace" (Romans 6:14). Likewise a Christian can continue to be sick after he has been born again but he doesn't have to be sick!

> *Who Himself bore our sins in His own body on the tree, that we, having died to sins, might live for righteousness – by whose stripes you are healed.*
>
> *(1 Peter 2:24)*

We have been redeemed from sickness! The price has been paid for our health. Therefore, sickness cannot exert dominion over us unless we allow it. Our faith will operate to the degree of our knowledge and application of God's Word and His covenant with us.

Friend, I will encourage you to meditate and confess these scriptures about the substitution of Jesus until the reality of your healing literally dominates your spirit, soul and body.

"For sin shall not have dominion over you, for you are not under law but under grace" (Romans 6:14). The power of the resurrection of Christ is at work within us, so a believer should not give up when he/she falls into sin. We are not under the law; to be under the law is to be under a system of trying to earn salvation in our own strength, by obeying the law.

However, to be under grace is to be justified and to live by the indwelling power of Christ. The Word of God says that we don't have to present our members as instruments of unrighteousness to sin:

And do not present your members as instruments of unrighteousness to sin, but present yourselves to God as being alive from the dead, and your members as instruments of righteousness to God.

(Romans 6:13)

The word *instruments* above means *weapon,* so if a believer sins; he/she gives a weapon to the devil in order to fight with them, which affects the *entire* body of Christ.

The Blood our Weapon

And war broke out in heaven: Michael and his angels fought with the dragon; and the dragon and his angels fought…

(Revelation 12:7)

Our revelation or knowledge of the Blood of Jesus Christ, gives us access and the upper hand over Satan. Our redemption and victory is in the Blood. Scripture says, there was war in heaven and they overcame the devil by the Blood (verse 11).

Satan and his followers did not find a place in heaven because the Lamb (Jesus) who was slain before the foundation of world, His blood, which was in heaven was deployed against Satan. The angels who overcame the devil applied the Blood.

And they overcame him by the blood of the Lamb and by the word of their testimony, and they did not love their lives to the death.

(Revelation 12:11)

Michael and his angels fought with the dragon; and the dragon and his angels fought back but the dragon did not prevail because of the Blood, which was deployed as a weapon against him.

So when the devil was cast out to the earth, God decided to transport the Blood, of His Son Jesus, to the earth. God deposited the Blood into the womb of a young virgin called Mary.

This was a mystery to Satan. God brought the Blood to the earth, so that His Children, the Christians, also could apply the Blood, the same way that Michael and his angels had used it as a weapon, against the dragon.

At Calvary, the Blood of Jesus was shed and when the Blood touched the earth there was an earthquake and rocks split. The purpose of the Blood coming to the earth was to defeat Satan and give the believer the access to use it as a weapon against the dragon.

The principle of the Blood and the believer is this; if the Christian fails to apply and to testify of the Blood, he/she can be defeated by the dragon. As Michael and his angels overcame him by the Blood, we also must overcome him with the Blood, by our faith in the Blood.

The Blood of Jesus still speaks for us. The bible says there are three things that bear witness in heaven and also three things that bear witness on the earth.

For there are three that bear witness in heaven: the Father, the Word, and the Holy Spirit; and these three are one. And there are three that bear witness on earth: the Spirit, the water, and the blood; and these three agree as one.

(1 John 5:7-8)

We have the Holy Spirit here on the earth because Jesus promised. "But when the Helper comes, whom I shall send to you from the Father, the Spirit of truth who proceeds from the Father, He will testify of Me" (John 15:26).

The Holy Spirit testifies concerning Christ at every point of His life. The Blood is both here and in heaven, to complete His redemption work. We have also the Word of God, the written Word to be applied as the sword of the Spirit, against the devil.

We are destined for victory through the Blood of the Lamb,

And they sang a new song, saying: "You are worthy to take the scroll, And to open its seals; For You were slain, and have redeemed us to God by Your blood out of every tribe and tongue and people and nation, And have made us kings and priests to our God; And we shall reign on the earth."

(Revelation 5:9-10)

❖

CHAPTER 8

The Covenant Table
and the Blood of Christ

When the Lord God wanted to deliver the Hebrews from Egypt, He needed an altar and the lamb. In this period of deliverance from Egypt, the blood sprinkled on the doorpost was symbolically the cross and the lamb. God told them to offer the lamb. It was an acceptable substitute for the entire nation.

> *Now the Lord spoke to Moses and Aaron in the land of Egypt, saying, "This month shall be your beginning of months; it shall be the first month of the year to you. Speak to all the congregation of Israel, saying: 'On the tenth day of this month every man shall take for himself a lamb, according to the house of his father, a lamb for a household.*

And if the household is too small for the lamb, let him and his neighbour next to his house take it according to the number of the persons; according to each man's need you shall make your count for the lamb. Your lamb shall be without blemish, a male of the first year. You may take it from the sheep or from the goats.'"

(Exodus 12:1-5)

God established the Passover meal as an ordinance to be kept from generation to generation. Since from the time God delivered the Hebrews from Egypt, they still celebrate the Passover because they shared the miraculous deliverance to their children's, children.

And it shall come to pass, when your children shall say unto you, What mean ye by this service? That ye shall say, It is the sacrifice of the Lord's passover, who passed over the houses of the children of Israel in Egypt, when he smote the Egyptians, and delivered our houses. And the people bowed the head and worshipped.

(Exodus 12:26-27 KJV)

The Cup of Blessing

There are requirements for the Lord's Supper. Here we see a parallel between the Old and the New Testaments. The first requirement was circumcision. This is an illustration for the cutting away of the old nature.

We do not practice *physical* circumcision. What they depicted *physically*, we now receive in Jesus Christ. It was mandatory that any man partaking of the Passover supper be circumcised:

In Him you were also circumcised with the circumcision made without hands, by putting off the body of the sins of the flesh, by the circumcision of Christ, buried with Him in baptism, in which you also were raised with Him through faith in the working of God, who raised Him from the dead.

And you, being dead in your trespasses and the uncircumcision of your flesh, He has made alive together with Him, having forgiven you all trespasses…
(Colossians 2:11-13)

There is a powerful aspect in the life of a Christian who partakes of the Lord's Table. There is a consequence to a believer who eats the communion of the Lord any how. "For this reason many *are* weak and sick among you, and many sleep" (1 Corinthians 11:30).

The bible says that we get sick and even die because we do not discern or understand the Lord's Body. We are advised to make self-examination in our hearts before coming to the Lord's Table. Self-examination simply means to confess your sins, repent and ask for forgiveness; then you can partake.

You must understand that the Lord's Supper is instituted and owned by Jesus Christ, our Lord. It is neither the church's supper nor man's supper. The Lord's Supper has been going on for over two thousand years. It is Jesus who decides who is eligible to partake; it's not the church leaders who decide.

We see through the scriptures that those who do partake are they that have a covenant with the Lord. Circumcision was the sign of the covenant. Every believer can conduct the Lord's Supper with his or her family but when it comes to the assembly of the Church it is the duty of the minister in charge to carry out or lead the Lord's Table.

There are a many beliefs and misconceptions about Holy Communion. People sometimes try to make it legalistic or make it so special, due to their position or calling. They can prepare it and send it across towns and nations to friends and loved ones because they perceive that their position can make the Holy Communion so special or more sanctified.

Due to lack of knowledge or deception, they forget that the Table is of the Lord and we partake by *faith*. We cannot invite people on the basis of our preference, since it is not *our* supper.

> *For I received from the Lord that which I also delivered to you: that the Lord Jesus on the same night in which He was betrayed took bread and when He had given thanks, He broke it and said, "Take, eat; this is My body which is broken for you; do this in remembrance of Me."*
>
> *In the same manner He also took the cup after supper, saying, "This cup is the new covenant in My blood. This do, as often as you drink it, in remembrance of Me." For as often as you eat this bread and drink this cup, you proclaim the Lord's death till He comes.*
> *(1 Corinthians 11:23-26)*

The communion declares our fellowship or union with the Lord Jesus. In the physical, it's true that you become what you eat. So also when you eat the Lord's Supper you would become more alive to remember His death and proclaim His gospel. Jesus has given us an obvious metaphor.

In the spiritual realm, we become like Jesus, when we partake of Him. In other words, you are what you eat spiritually. When we physically partake of the Lord's Supper, we are declaring that we are one with Him. If you eat of the bread and drink of the cup, just like any ordinary food and drink, then it means nothing.

I am not saying that the bread and cup are literally and chemically the Body and Blood of Jesus! But I am saying that by *faith,* as we partake of the communion, the very *presence* of Jesus is in the communion. As we eat, we are declaring, "I am one with Christ Jesus."

> *I have been crucified with Christ; it is no longer I who live, but Christ lives in me; and the life which I now live in the flesh I live by faith in the Son of God, who loved me and gave Himself for me.*
>
> (Galatians 2:20)

❖

Bibliography

- Strong, James. S.T.D., L.L.D. 1890. <u>Strong's Exhaustive Concordance; Dictionaries of the Hebrew and Greek Words</u>. e-Sword ® version 7.6.1 Copyright © 2000-2005. All Rights Reserved. Registered trade mark of Rick Meyers. Equipping Ministries Foundation. USA www.e-sword.net.

- Unless otherwise indicated, all scriptural quotations are taken from the New King James Version®. Copyright © 1982 by Thomas Nelson, Inc. Used by permission. All rights reserved.

- Scripture references marked ESV are taken from the ESV® Bible (The Holy Bible, English Standard Version®), copyright © 2001 by Crossway, a publishing ministry of Good News Publishers. Used by permission. All rights reserved.

- Scripture references marked KJV are taken from the King James Version of the bible.

- Scripture references marked NIV are taken from The Holy Bible, New International Version® NIV®. Copyright © 1973, 1978, 1984, 2011 by Biblica, Inc.™ Used by permission of Zondervan Publishing House. All rights reserved worldwide.

❖

Ministry Profile
Apostle Dr Benjamin Ayim Asare

Dr. Benjamin Ayim Asare is an anointed minister of God with a strong deliverance flow, which is evident in all facets of his ministry. He is the president of **World Missions Ministries (WMM)** and the Senior Pastor of the **Followers of Christ International Church (FOCIC)** Novara, Italy.

Apostle Benjamin is the coordinator and the vice president of the Followers of Christ International Church. A member of **"Chiese Elim in Italia"** and holds Italian Ministerial Licenses "Ministro di culto." He is also on the Executive Board of Alan Pateman Ministries (APMI), a Trustee, and Vice President of Lifestyle International Christian University (LICU), where he holds the position of Faculty Member, Professor of Theology and National Director for Ghana, being responsible for National Growth.

Furthermore Dr. Benjamin is an Executive Board Member of the International Apostolic Accreditation Council (IAAC) where he is overseeing the Association of Professionals (May 7th, 2013).

Dr. Benjamin is a conference speaker, church planter, leadership mentor. He is an itinerant minister who ministers to organizations as well as groups and churches and ministers throughout nations.

In May 2010 Apostle Ayim Asare established the **"School of Ministry for Potential Leaders" (SOMFPL)** the aim is to provide training/seminar programs for ordinary people to potential leaders for the work of ministry, and that is to help them to identify their calling and ministry. This is the purpose and burden of the pastor and his leaders.

Dr. Benjamin is the owner of **"BENCOM Publication,"** publishing and distribution materials such as "Salvation is Free" for churches as Sunday school tools in English and in Italian and has authored several books.

This anointed man of God encourages thousands to answer the call of God through the teaching of the Word and dynamic demonstration of the Holy Spirit. His unique ability to identify the God-given gifting, calling and anointing upon God's people, through his proven dynamic teachings, draws the hearts of the people to our Lord and Saviour Jesus Christ as God's purpose is activated in their lives. Clearly, minds are renewed, lives are transformed and hearts are drawn to our heavenly Father as God's power and authority is magnificently displayed.

Apostle Dr. Benjamin Ayim Asare lives in Novara, Italy with his family.

www.benjaminayimasareministries.com
bayimasare@yahoo.it
focicatmissions@yahoo.com

❖

To Contact the Author

Please email:

Followers of Christ International Church
c/o Apostle Benjamin Ayim Asare
Via Ghiberti, 1
Novara 28100
ITALY

Email: bayimasare@yahoo.it or
focicatmissions@yahoo.com

*Please include your prayer requests
and comments when you write.*

❖

Other Books

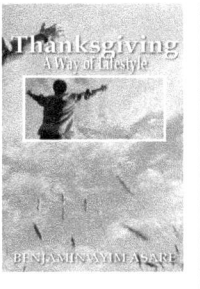

Thanksgiving, A Way of Lifestyle

Within this book, Apostle Benjamin Ayim Asare will help you to discover the importance of thanksgiving and every bumped crop you have attained in life. You will also discover how to appreciate people whom God uses to bless your life. Everything we enjoy in the present and coming age is a gift from God worthy of thanksgiving. All people including non Christians and Christians enjoy the blessings of the Lord.

ISBN: 978-0-9575775-2-7, Pages: 92,
Format: Paperback, Published: 2017

Discover your Ministry in the Local Church

When you begin to develop the ability to sever all alternatives and give total concentration and focus to the things that interests you most, you will discover incredible and remarkable success. Dr. Benjamin Ayim has provided a tool which will open your understanding to discover the purpose, the need and the practical approach of the ministry of helps in the local church.

ISBN: 978-0-9575775-1-0, Pages: 153,
Format: Paperback, Published: 2016

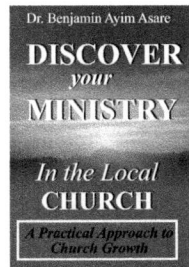

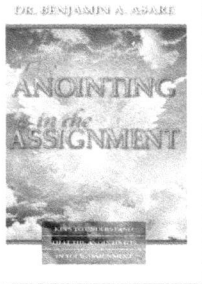

The Anointing is in the Assignment

The purpose of the anointing is for you as a Christian to live a victorious life and to witness the gospel message of Jesus Christ effectively. God wants to take ordinary people and work supernaturally through them to bring about a mighty move of His power, just the way He worked through His Son, Jesus Christ.

ISBN: 978-1-909132-07-8, Pages: 220,
Format: Paperback, Published: 2015

The Hand of the Diligent Will Rule

God has given us His resources of Time and Talent to receive money. You must remember that work is important to God. God values the work you do, because your work or job is equal to your time, talent and gifting. These gifts are God's resources and therefore God will not be happy with any of His children who take work for granted. Your work requires diligence, and excellent attitude determines good quality productivity.

ISBN: 978-0-957577-50-3, Pages: 120,
Format: Paperback, Published: 2013

Life is a Priceless Treasure

As you look beyond your time on earth, which in comparison with eternity, is just a brief moment, you will be assured that heaven, is your home. Time spent on earth is short. Yet this short time is very essential because it prepares you to receive everything needed in heaven.

BENCOM Publications, Pages: 47,
Format: Paperback, Published: 2008

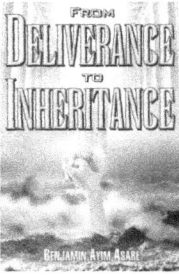

From Deliverance to Inheritance

In this revolutionary book on deliverance, you will discover, understand and know the enemy, and know how you can take your strength in the Lord to overcome him in order to possess your inheritance.

BENCOM Publications, Pages: 129,
Format: Paperback, Published: 2008

- Italian Books -

La Vita è un Tesoro Inestimabile

Quando guardi al di là del tuo tempo sulla terra, che in confronto all' eternità è solo un breve momento, sarai sicuro che il cielo sarà la tua casa. Il tempo vissuto sulla terra è breve. Tuttavia, questi breve periodo di tempo è una cosa molto indispensabile, perchè ti prepara a ricevere tuute le cose di cui hai bisogno nel cielo.

ISBN 978-88-87511-90-1, Pages: 44,
Format: Paperback, Published: 2009

Dalla Liberazione all'Eredità

Libertà significa semplicemente uscire da una prigione o da problemi di legami economici, sociali e politici. Gesù fu mandato intenzionalmente da Dio per liberarci dal dominio del nemico.

ISBN 978-88-87511-85-7, Pages: 96,
Format: Paperback, Published: 2009

www.ingramcontent.com/pod-product-compliance
Lightning Source LLC
Chambersburg PA
CBHW071454070426
42452CB00039B/1358